Original title:
When Nighttime Giggles Bloom

Copyright © 2024 Creative Arts Management OÜ
All rights reserved.

Author: Dorian Ashford
ISBN HARDBACK: 978-9916-90-500-5
ISBN PAPERBACK: 978-9916-90-501-2

Whispers of the Moonlit Laughter

In silver beams the night awakes,
Soft giggles echo, the stillness breaks.
Beneath the sky's embracing glow,
Whispers dance where moonlight flows.

Stars listen close, their secrets shared,
In shadows deep, no heart feels scared.
With every laugh, the darkness flees,
A melody carried on the breeze.

Shadows Dance in Joyful Pairs

In twilight's charm, the shadows sway,
Two figures glide, lost in their play.
The world falls silent, just them and night,
In each small movement, hearts take flight.

Laughter twirls like autumn leaves,
In whispered stories, love believes.
They spin and laugh, a sweet embrace,
Eclipsing fears with their joyous grace.

Midnight Murmurs of Delight

By light of stars, soft voices hum,
In every note, the secrets come.
Through tangled dreams, they gently flow,
Midnight murmurs of lovers know.

In secret glades where wishes bloom,
The night enfolds, dispelling gloom.
With every sigh, the heavens sigh,
As tender whispers fill the sky.

Starlit Chuckles in the Dark

Amidst the night, the starlight plays,
With chuckles bright in shadowy bays.
Each flicker holds a tale so bold,
Of laughter shared and dreams retold.

In cosmic winks, the universe beams,
Reflecting joy in whispered dreams.
With every twinkle, hope ignites,
In starlit chuckles, the heart delights.

The Playfulness of Evening Tides

Waves dance lightly on the shore,
Soft whispers from the ocean's core.
Colors mingle, orange and blue,
As dusk unfurls her satin hue.

Children laugh, their footprints fade,
In the sandy games they've played.
The tide rolls in, a gentle tease,
Embracing all with playful ease.

The moon peeks out, a silver thread,
Weaving dreams in twilight's bed.
Stars begin to twinkle bright,
Guiding hearts into the night.

Nature sighs, a soothing balm,
Cradling earth in evening's calm.
In this moment, peace resides,
With the playfulness of evening tides.

Giggling Stars and Wandering Thoughts

In the velvet sky above,
Stars twinkle with a giggling love.
Thoughts meander, wild and free,
Chasing shadows, light as glee.

Constellations weave their tales,
Sailing through the cosmic gales.
The moonlight laughs in soft delight,
Guiding dreams in the still of night.

Whispers of the universe call,
Inviting all to heed its thrall.
With every twinkle, secrets shared,
In this wonder, we are bared.

Wandering thoughts like rivers flow,
In starry laughter, we let go.
For in the night, we're not alone,
With giggling stars, we find our home.

Celestial Laughter's Gentle Touch

In the stillness of the night,
Celestial laughter takes its flight.
Stars sprinkle joy with every gleam,
Awakening the heart's deep dream.

Heaven's whispers, soft and bright,
Dancing shadows in fading light.
Every twinkling, every sigh,
Reminds us of the why and by.

The cosmos hums a tender tune,
Beneath the watchful, silvery moon.
With every pulse, the heart aligns,
In gentle laughter, love defines.

As constellations weave their thread,
Softly guiding where we're led.
In this embrace, our spirits clutch,
The warmth of celestial laughter's touch.

Twilight's Secret Symphony of Joy

As twilight wraps the world in grace,
A secret symphony takes its place.
Notes of laughter fill the air,
With melodies beyond compare.

Shadows dance to the evening song,
In harmony, where we belong.
The horizon blushes, deep and warm,
Creating magic with its charm.

The stars awaken, one by one,
While the last rays of the day are done.
Moonlight spills its silver flow,
In twilight's joy, our spirits glow.

Feel the heartbeat of the night,
In silence, find your true delight.
With every note, the heart will soar,
Twilight's symphony, forevermore.

Hues of Glee Beneath Twilight

Brushstrokes of orange fade to blue,
Dancing whispers in the evening dew.
Echoes of laughter fill the air,
Colors entwine without a care.

Stars begin to twinkle above,
Signaling the night's gentle shove.
Hearts open wide with pure delight,
Embracing the magic of twilight.

Laughter's Echoes in Quiet Hours

In the hush of the waning day,
Laughter echoes in soft ballet.
Memories weave through shadows cast,
Moments like shadows, fading fast.

The clock ticks softly as dreams fly,
Underneath the velvet sky.
With every sigh of tranquil night,
Laughter lingers, a soft light.

Secret Smiles of the Night Sky

Beneath the blanket of midnight hue,
Stars are secrets known to few.
Glimmers of hope in each bright spark,
Whispers of dreams in the dark.

Clouds drift softly like gentle sighs,
Embracing the wishes, as time flies.
Radiance beams on hidden fates,
Creating a wonder that never waits.

Nocturnal Joys in Silken Dreams

In the realm where moonbeams play,
Night reveals its soft array.
Silken dreams and shadows blend,
As worries fade and spirits mend.

A tapestry of starry lights,
Fills the air with sweet delights.
Slumber wraps the world in peace,
Nocturnal joys that never cease.

Evening's Playful Haunt

Shadows dance as daylight fades,
Whispers soft beneath the glades.
Crickets chirp in sweet refrain,
Echoes wrap the night in chain.

Glimmers flash on the pond's face,
Nature's laughter fills the space.
Fireflies twinkle in delight,
As the world surrenders night.

Moonbeams brush the woodland trees,
Swaying gently in the breeze.
Stars emerge, a shining fleet,
Dancing softly to the beat.

In this realm of shadowed grace,
Evening's charm, a sweet embrace.
Magic weaves through dark and light,
In the arms of tranquil night.

Moonlit Mirth

Underneath the glowing moon,
Nighttime's laughter starts to croon.
Waves of joy on silver beams,
Weaving softly through our dreams.

Laughter echoes through the trees,
Carried forward by the breeze.
Whirling clouds in playful flight,
We grow brighter in the night.

Stars align, a twinkling crowd,
Gathering, their laughter loud.
In this world of mystic cheer,
Even shadows draw so near.

Moonlit pranks ignite the air,
Joy and wonder everywhere.
Underneath this endless sky,
Hearts uplifted, spirits fly.

Luminous Laughter in the Twilight

Twilight spills like molten gold,
Stories of the night unfold.
Whispers dance upon the breeze,
Bringing warmth with perfect ease.

Laughter sparkles in the air,
Coloring the world with flair.
As the sun begins to dip,
Moons await a joyful trip.

In the garden shadows play,
Fireflies join the grand ballet.
Each smile casts a luminous hue,
Painting night with joy anew.

As the stars begin to gleam,
We embrace this vivid dream.
Moments treasured, spirits bright,
In the laughter of the night.

Stars Wink and Giggle

Up above, the heavens sigh,
Stars wink down from vaults so high.
In the hush of night's embrace,
They giggle softly, full of grace.

Twinkling lights like secrets shared,
In the darkness, brightly bared.
Constellations weave a tale,
Filling hearts with joy that sail.

Galaxies in playful spree,
Painting dreams, so wild and free.
Each glance a spark, a silent cheer,
Echoes of what we hold dear.

With each blink, they send a wish,
A cosmic dance, a timeless swish.
Underneath the stellar show,
Hearts expand, and spirits glow.

The Softness of Nighttime Humor

The moonlight glows with a gentle grin,
Whispers of laughter cradled within.
Stars twinkle softly, sharing their glee,
A nighttime jest from the cosmos, you see.

Crickets join in, their music a tease,
While shadows dance playfully among the trees.
Chasing the worries that daylight has spun,
Beneath the cool sky, we're all just for fun.

A chuckle from afar, a giggle so bright,
The warmth of the night wraps us up tight.
In this hush of the dark, all troubles take flight,
Together we revel in the softness of night.

Chirps and Chuckles in the Twilight

As day bids farewell, a soft song begins,
With chirps and chuckles, the evening spins.
A chorus of critters, their humor so grand,
In twilight's embrace, together we stand.

The breeze carries laughter, so light and so free,
With each little flutter, joy flows like a sea.
Dancing on air, the whispers ignite,
Filling the dusk with delight and goodnight.

Fireflies flicker, their glow like a wink,
In this magic moment, we pause and we think.
Of shared little secrets, and dreams that unite,
In chirps and chuckles that echo the night.

Mirthful Breezes Through Silvery Trees

Breezes swirl gently, with laughter in tow,
Through silver-leafed branches, they whisper and flow.
Soft rustling sounds weave tales in the dark,
As leaves share their giggles, a shimmering spark.

The night hums along, in sweet playful tunes,
Charmed by the glow of the watching moon.
Mirth dances lightly, on the edges of dreams,
With the cool, silken air, laughter softly teems.

In the stillness we gather, beneath ancient trees,
With hearts full of wonder, riding night's gentle breeze.
The joy is contagious, in this haven we find,
Mirthful breezes a balm for the mind.

Secrets Shared Under Moonlight

Beneath the moon's gaze, with secrets in hand,
We whisper our hopes in this night's quiet land.
The stars bear witness to dreams that we weave,
In shadows and murmurs, our souls gently cleave.

A rustle of leaves, as laughter spills free,
In this sacred moment, just you, and just me.
Under the soft glow, we share what we keep,
Stories like treasures, our bond running deep.

The night cradles whispers, soft as a sigh,
With twilight's embrace, we let go and fly.
In secrets on moonbeams, our spirits will twine,
Forever encircled, your heart next to mine.

The Enchanted Hour of Laughter

In twilight's glow, the laughter flows,
Like gentle ripples where joy bestows.
With friends around, the troubles cease,
In merriment, we find our peace.

The clock strikes soft, our spirits rise,
As giggles weave beneath the skies.
In every joke, a world takes flight,
In this enchanted hour of light.

The flickering candles cast their charms,
Drawing close in each other's arms.
A symphony of mirth and cheer,
In this moment, we hold dear.

Through laughter's dance, our hearts ignite,
We chase away the creeping night.
With every grin, our burdens fray,
In this hour, we forever stay.

Nocturnal Whimsy

Beneath the stars, the world spins round,
In dreams of whimsy, magic's found.
The moonlight whispers, secrets bright,
As shadows play in silver light.

In quiet corners, laughter grows,
With each soft giggle, the night bestows.
In gentle breezes, tales unfold,
Of nocturnal wonders, bold and gold.

The owls converse in playful jest,
As fireflies twinkle, their tiny quest.
Each moment holds a spark of glee,
In this realm of mystery.

The night unfolds, a canvas wide,
With every heartbeat, side by side.
In whimsical dance, we find our way,
In nocturnal dreams, forever stay.

Chuckles in the Celestial Night

A billion stars begin to smile,
Inviting us to stay awhile.
In cosmic jest, the laughter flows,
With every twinkle, merriment grows.

The planets wink in playful glee,
As comets dash in jubilee.
In the silence of the velvet sky,
We share our secrets, you and I.

The darkness holds a soothing sound,
As chuckles echo all around.
In the embrace of night's delight,
We dance beneath the stellar light.

With every joke, the silence breaks,
In laughter's warmth, the cosmos wakes.
In celestial realms, our spirits soar,
In chuckles shared, we find much more.

The Gleeful Dance of Shadows

When daylight fades, the shadows rise,
In jolly leaps beneath the skies.
They twirl and sway, a playful band,
In the twilight's glow, hand in hand.

A gleeful dance, a jester's play,
As evening calls, we drift away.
With every flicker, our laughter rings,
As night unfolds and joy takes wing.

In whispered tones, the shadows prance,
Each step they take, a fleeting chance.
Through alleyways and moonlit paths,
We join the dance, dispelling wrath.

With every twist, the night embraces,
In merry heartbeats, we find our places.
In this gleeful dance, let shadows swirl,
For in their laughter, we too twirl.

The Giggles of Dreams in Stillness

In the hush of twilight's glow,
Laughter dances soft and low.
A whisper winds through slumber's gate,
Where dreams and giggles gently wait.

Stars peek in, their glimmers bright,
Casting shadows, soft and light.
In moonlit fields, the laughter flies,
As dreams take shape in starlit skies.

Echoes of Joy Beneath the Stars

Beneath the night, where dreams collide,
Echoes of laughter swell with pride.
In the embrace of the cool night's air,
Joy found in moments, tender and rare.

Whispers of wishes fly on high,
As secrets weave through the velvet sky.
With each twinkle, a story unfolds,
Of hearts in harmony and dreams untold.

Frolicsome Whispers in the Night Air

In the stillness, whispers twine,
Playful spirits, a dance divine.
The breeze carries tales of delight,
Frolicsome echoes in the night.

Laughter cascades through branches thin,
As joy sets free what once had been.
In shadows deep, the secrets play,
While the moon watches, bright as day.

Mischief and Merriment at Midnight

At the stroke of midnight's cheer,
Mischief brews, bringing near.
Laughter bubbles like a stream,
As night unfurls its whimsical dream.

Stars twinkle, join the fun,
In the jest of moon and sun.
In every corner, joy ignites,
Creating magic on lonely nights.

Sprite's Laughter in the Dim Light

In shadows play the sprites so bright,
They twirl and laugh, a pure delight.
With whispers soft, they weave their charm,
In every flicker, there's no harm.

Underneath the stars they find their dance,
In gentle breeze, they take a chance.
Their giggles echo through the trees,
As night wraps all in tranquil ease.

With every leap and bound they make,
The world around begins to wake.
In dim light glows their joyful spree,
A secret world, just them and me.

So linger here where shadows play,
With sprites who laugh till break of day.
They shimmer bright, a vision rare,
In the twilight, light as air.

Dances of Delight Beneath the Moon

Beneath the moon, the dancers sway,
In silver light, they find their way.
With joy unbound, they spin and twirl,
A magical night, a wondrous whirl.

The stars above watch in delight,
As rhythms blend with the soft night light.
A symphony of joy they weave,
In every breath, a gift to receive.

They leap with mirth, their spirits free,
In every glance, a sweet decree.
Together lost in pure embrace,
Each moment cherished in this place.

As night unfolds, the music calls,
In whispered tones and gentle thralls.
With every beat, their hearts ignite,
In dances bright beneath the night.

Mirthful Murmurs of the Night Sky

The night sky hums a cheerful tune,
With stars that wink, and the glowing moon.
Each whisper tells of dreams so grand,
In every twinkle, hope takes hand.

Clouds drift by with a gentle grace,
As playful winds begin to race.
A tapestry of joy unfolds,
In tales of wonder, softly told.

With every sigh, the cosmos gleams,
In quiet hours, we weave our dreams.
The laughter lingers, soft and bright,
In the mirthful murmurs of the night.

So close your eyes, and feel the glow,
Let starlit whispers softly flow.
In this embrace, the heart shall soar,
Through mirthful skies forevermore.

Joyful Whispers in the Night Air

In the gentle night, dreams take flight,
Softly dancing in the silver light.
Stars above wink with delight,
Embracing shadows, pure and bright.

Laughter weaves through darkened trees,
Carried on a playful breeze.
Whispers echo, full of cheer,
As joy surrounds, we hold it near.

Hearts entwined in this twilight glow,
Sowing seeds of love to grow.
Each breath a promise, sweet embrace,
In the night's warmth, we find our place.

As the moon watches from on high,
We weave our dreams, let our spirits fly.
Joyful whispers, soft and clear,
In the night air, we have no fear.

Midnight Revelries

Underneath a velvet sky,
Mysteries in shadows lie.
Candles flicker, hearts align,
In the dark, our spirits shine.

Laughter spills like starry light,
Moments cherished in the night.
Whispers dance on silver streams,
Revelries born from secret dreams.

Time suspends in midnight's thrill,
Every heartbeat, every chill.
Joy entwined with shadows' play,
Magic beckons, come what may.

As the hours softly fade,
Promises of dreams we've made.
In these moments, we find grace,
Midnight's revels, our sacred space.

The Mischievous Moon

High above with a knowing smile,
The moon winks, embracing style.
Casting shadows, playful beams,
Stirring up our wildest dreams.

Tickling laughter in the night,
Drawing secrets into light.
Whispers carried on the breeze,
The moon plays with the swaying trees.

Each glow a secret, soft and sly,
Winking stars are standing by.
In this game of light and play,
Mischief found in night's ballet.

So let us dance under her glow,
In moonlit chaos, let love flow.
With every heartbeat, truth unfurls,
Among the dreams, we share our worlds.

Murmurs of Joy in the Dark

Silence blankets the sleeping ground,
In the dark, soft joys abound.
Murmured laughter fills the air,
Crafting moments rich and rare.

Secrets shared with a gentle sigh,
Underneath the starry sky.
Echoes of love intertwine,
As shadows dance, hearts align.

With every heartbeat, hope ignites,
Illuminating silent nights.
In the peace, we find our way,
Murmurs brightening the gray.

As the world sleeps, we ignite,
The spark of joy in the night.
Together in this calm embrace,
Murmurs of joy, a timeless space.

Moonbeams Crafting Whimsy

In silver hues, the moonlight glows,
Whispers softly where soft wind blows.
Dancing shadows play on the ground,
In this gentle night, magic's found.

Dreams take flight on beams so bright,
Crafting stories through the night.
Laughter echoes, sweet and clear,
As moonbeams weave our dreams, so near.

Bright-eyed owls hoot their soft tune,
Under the watch of a gleaming moon.
Stars wink above in playful glee,
Nature's smile is wild and free.

With every twinkle, hearts align,
In a world where shadows shine.
Moonbeams twirl with joyful grace,
Whimsy dances in this sacred space.

Enchanted Giggles Beneath the Veil

Beneath the veil of soft twilight,
Gentle giggles dance in flight.
Fireflies twinkle, a gentle spark,
Lighting up the paths so dark.

Whispers of dreams drift through the air,
Magic flickers everywhere.
Stars above begin to sing,
Woven tales the night will bring.

In secret groves where shadows twine,
Children's laughter, sweet as wine.
Fairies flit on wings so light,
Painting joy in the heart of night.

Together we weave a tapestry bright,
Of enchanted giggles that take to flight.
Under the moon, we laugh and play,
Embraced by magic till break of day.

The Serenade of Sleepy Grins

Softly the world begins to fade,
As dreams arise in twilight's shade.
Sleepy grins on every face,
Wrapped in warmth, in love's embrace.

The stars above hum a lullaby,
As moonlight paints the night sky.
In gentle whispers, secrets shared,
A serenade for hearts that dared.

Pillows cradle thoughts divine,
While shadows dance, the dreams align.
Resting souls drift far away,
In sleepy grins, the night will play.

Time stands still, as heartbeats hum,
To the melodies that softly come.
The world outside will fade from view,
In serenades that feel so true.

Night's Canvas Painted with Joy

On night's canvas, colors swirl,
With shades of wonder, dreams unfurl.
Brushstrokes of laughter fill the air,
A masterpiece beyond compare.

Each twinkling star, a joyful spark,
Creating scenes where magic's dark.
Whispers of night blend hopes and dreams,
In this place where starlight beams.

Moonlit pathways pave the way,
For heart's delights in soft array.
Joy spills over, bright and bold,
As stories of night gently unfold.

In vivid hues, the night is alive,
A canvas where our spirits thrive.
With every breath, joy's colors blend,
In night's embrace, our hearts transcend.

The Delighted Nightingale

In the garden where dreams take flight,
A nightingale sings under soft moonlight.
Her melody flows like a gentle stream,
Casting shadows of beauty over the dream.

With each note, the flowers do sway,
Whispering secrets of the end of day.
Buds unfold in the tender glow,
As the nightingale dances, stealing the show.

Charmed by the magic of her sweet song,
The stars twinkle brightly, where they belong.
In a world where the silence speaks,
An enchanting chorus of nature's peaks.

So she sings until the dawn's bright light,
Filling the air with her pure delight.
In every heart, her song finds a home,
The delighted nightingale, forever to roam.

Midnight Laughter's Embrace

Beneath the cloak of the midnight sky,
Laughter dances and spirits fly.
Echoing softly through the quiet night,
A symphony of joy, pure and bright.

Moonbeams waltz, casting playful glows,
As whispers of secrets from the shadows grow.
Hands intertwined, friends gather near,
The warmth of laughter erases all fear.

With each shared story, dreams take flight,
In the embrace of the soft, starlit night.
Time stands still as the world fades away,
Lost in the joy, come what may.

At dawn's first blush, the laughter will fade,
Yet memories linger in the promises made.
In the heart's quiet corner, it will always stay,
Midnight laughter's embrace, forever at play.

Playful Shadows at Evening's Gate

As the sun dips low, the shadows grow,
Dancing lightly where soft winds blow.
Flickering forms paint the earth,
Whispering secrets of twilight's birth.

At evening's gate, mischief takes flight,
Shadows frolic, bidding day goodnight.
They spin and twirl in the fading light,
In a world alive with pure delight.

From tree to tree, they roam and play,
Carving laughter from the close of day.
With every flicker, a story untold,
In shades of mystery, brave and bold.

As night wraps the world in its cloak,
The playful shadows continue to stoke.
With twilight's brush, they softly unite,
Creating a canvas of wonder and light.

Whimsy in the Stars' Light

In the depths of the night, where wonders gleam,
The stars offer whispers, a whimsical dream.
Each twinkle a tale from far-off places,
In the celestial dance, joy softly embraces.

Riding on comets, laughter does soar,
Unraveling mysteries forevermore.
Serenading the heavens with dreams untold,
The magic of starlight is a sight to behold.

With a wink and a nod, the cosmos sings,
Inviting us all to spread our wings.
Under this canvas, our hearts ignite,
In the infinite embrace of the stars' light.

So let us wander through this cosmic sea,
Finding whimsy in all that can be.
For in every shimmer, in each fleeting glance,
There lies a chance for the heart to dance.

Palettes of Laughter Under Velvet Skies

Colors dance like fireflies,
Joy spills across the night,
Each giggle a brushstroke,
Under stars, hearts take flight.

Whispers weave through the air,
As dreams begin to twirl,
In the canvas of the dark,
Laughter paints the world.

Velvet skies hold secrets,
As we play in sweet delight,
In the glow of our smiles,
The universe feels right.

With each burst of chuckles,
The worries fade away,
In this art of connection,
We find our joyful sway.

Joy Sprouts in the Cool Night Air.

In the hush of nightfall,
Soft laughter fills the breeze,
Joy blooms like flowers,
In shadows of the trees.

Stars twinkle like lanterns,
Guiding dreams with their light,
Each chuckle a melody,
Echoing through the night.

Whispers of friendship grow,
Rooted deep in our hearts,
In this garden of laughter,
New magic always starts.

Underneath the moon's glow,
Hope and light gently blend,
In the cool, sweet night air,
Our spirits upward send.

Laughter Under the Moonlight

Moonlight washes over us,
With a silver, tender touch,
Laughter flutters lightly,
We savor every much.

In this soft, shining glow,
Shadows dance on the ground,
Every giggle twinkles bright,
In this moment, we're found.

Facing the gleam of the stars,
We share secrets divine,
In the warmth of our joy,
Together, we brightly shine.

Echoes of sweet laughter,
Drift softly through the night,
Under the moon's embrace,
Everything feels just right.

Whispers of the Starlit Hours

In the hush of starlit hours,
Whispers float like a sigh,
Laughter weaves through the night,
As constellations fly.

Joy lingers in the darkness,
Like fireflies in the air,
Each chuckle a treasure,
A memory that we share.

Hope sparkles above us,
Guiding our playful hearts,
In this tapestry of dreams,
Joy crafts its own fine arts.

With every laugh and whisper,
The night wraps us so tight,
In the embrace of the stars,
We dance until the light.

The Delightful Art of Nocturnal Play

In shadows deep where whispers sigh,
The moonlight dances, a lullaby.
Creatures stir in soft, sweet delight,
Chasing dreams in the cloak of night.

Stars flicker like eyes, twinkling bright,
As joy unfolds in the velvet light.
Nature hums a tune, soft and clear,
A melody only nightlings hear.

With each rustle, a story's spun,
Underneath the watchful sun.
In this realm, we are free to roam,
Finding magic, our heart's true home.

The world asleep, yet we arise,
Crafting moments under starlit skies.
A playful dance, timeless and grand,
In the delightful night, hand in hand.

Joy Unveiled in Twilight

As day bows down to twilight's grace,
A gentle smile takes night's embrace.
Colors blend in a soft serenade,
Whispers of joy in twilight fade.

Laughter echoes through dusky air,
Hearts unburdened, free from care.
The horizon glows in shades of gold,
A story of joy waiting to unfold.

In the hush, our spirits soar,
Embracing moments, forevermore.
With each flicker, the light will wane,
Yet joy remains, our sweet refrain.

So let us dance in the fading light,
Celebrating all that feels so right.
Twilight's song, a tender embrace,
A joyful heart in a tranquil space.

Charms of the Nocturnal Ballet

In the garden where moonbeams twirl,
Night's dancers spin, a dreamlike whirl.
Owls hoot softly, a watchful gaze,
As delicate wings grace the night's haze.

Beneath the boughs of ancient trees,
A balmy breeze brings whispered pleas.
Fireflies flicker, tiny stars aglow,
Guiding our steps in the shadow's flow.

With every leap, the heart takes flight,
Joined in this charming, tranquil night.
The silent music swells, it sways,
Enchanting souls in twilight's plays.

Together we glide, lost in the trance,
Enthralled by the nocturnal dance.
In this ballet where dreams unite,
We find our joy in the still of night.

Serene Laughter Among the Stars

Beneath the canopy of night so vast,
Laughter weaves through moments that pass.
With every chuckle, the stars align,
Creating magic, your hand in mine.

The world quiets down, yet our hearts race,
As we share secrets in this sacred space.
Echoes of joy ripple through the air,
Dancing with starlight without a care.

In the cool embrace of the evening's song,
We celebrate where we both belong.
Every twinkle, a wink from afar,
Inviting us closer, among the stars.

So let our laughter ring out so clear,
A melody cherished, drawing near.
In the galaxy's arms, pure bliss we find,
Serene laughter, in starlit kind.

Moonbeams and Mischief

In the silent night so bright,
Whispers dance on silver light.
Starlit shadows guide my way,
Through the laughter of the sway.

Laughter echoes in the gloom,
While the twilight starts to bloom.
Mischief hides in every glance,
Inviting dreams to take a chance.

Moonbeams spill on sleeping trees,
Breezes sing with gentle ease.
In this world of soft delight,
Magic dances, pure and light.

Every glance, a little thrill,
Joy ignites, the heart does fill.
In this night where dreams can roam,
Moonlit mischief finds a home.

Silhouettes of Joy in the Dark

In the shadows, laughter plays,
Joyful hearts set forth to blaze.
Silhouettes in twilight's grace,
Every smile, a warm embrace.

Stars above, a twinkling cheer,
Filling hearts with dreams so dear.
In the quiet, we unite,
Finding joy in distant light.

Whispers echo through the trees,
Carried softly by the breeze.
In the dark, we spin and twirl,
Silhouettes in evening's whirl.

Every heartbeat shares a song,
In this place where we belong.
Dance with shadows, lose the fright,
Silhouettes of joy ignite.

Midnight's Delicate Laughter

Midnight laughs, a gentle sound,
Rippling through the quiet ground.
Stars burst forth in playful beams,
As we wander, lost in dreams.

Every moment carries light,
Softly stitched in endless night.
Laughter dances on the air,
Chasing shadows everywhere.

Whispers blend with moonlit sighs,
Filling hearts with tender highs.
In this twilight, spirits soar,
Midnight's laughter, evermore.

So let us play, no time to waste,
In this dream, we are embraced.
Delicate in every sound,
Midnight's joy forever found.

Fancies Shining in the Night

Fancies twinkle, stars align,
In the night where dreams define.
Every wish is but a thread,
Woven softly in our head.

Chasing whispers in the dark,
Finding life in every spark.
Moonlit visions draw us near,
Fancies blooming, bright and clear.

Shadows dance with playful grace,
In this wondrous, secret space.
Every heartbeat sings a tune,
Beneath the glow of silver moon.

Let us wander hand in hand,
Through this gentle, twilight land.
Fancies shining, hearts unite,
In the magic of the night.

The Night's Giggling Tapestry

In shadows we weave, laughter's soft thread,
Whispers of secrets, where dreams are fed.
Stars twinkle brightly, in night's gentle arms,
Embracing the magic, of childhood's charms.

A dance of the fireflies, in playful delight,
They twirl and they flicker, in the hush of the night.
Each giggle a melody, lost in the breeze,
As the moon casts a glow, through whispering trees.

In corners of twilight, joy starts to bloom,
With every soft chuckle, dispelling the gloom.
The night wraps around us, like a warm caress,
In this giggling tapestry, we find happiness.

So let laughter linger, in this starlit expanse,
As we share in the magic, in a playful dance.
A tapestry woven, of dreams and of mirth,
In the heart of the night, we find our true worth.

Fantasies at the Edge of Darkness

At the brink of twilight, where shadows play,
Fantasies flicker, like whispers of day.
A realm full of wonder, where spirits fly high,
Holding onto our dreams, as they bloom in the sky.

In the silence of nightfall, hopes softly soar,
Beneath the vast heavens, we yearn for much more.
Each thought a confetti, in the still of the hour,
As we dive into dreams, as they blossom like flower.

Through the misty adventures, our hearts intertwine,
In the realm of the nighttime, where stars brightly shine.
We dance with the shadows, in a waltz of delight,
Fantasies bloom, as we hold on so tight.

Let the darkness envelop, like a comforting shroud,
Crafting our stories, both tender and loud.
In this embrace of the night, we find our true song,
Fantasies sparkle, where dreams can belong.

Echoing Laughter Beneath the Stars

Under the vast sky, where the stars gleam bright,
Echoes of laughter fade into the night.
Joy dances with shadows, as memories weave,
A tapestry of moments that never deceive.

With each joyful echo, a story unfolds,
Whispers of laughter, in the night so bold.
The moon is a keeper, of tales lost in time,
As we share in the moments, so sweet and sublime.

Around campfires crackling, we gather so near,
Voices rise up, filling the air with cheer.
In the glow of the embers, friendships ignite,
With echoing laughter, we embrace the night.

Beneath the vast stars, our dreams come alive,
Echoing laughter, is where joy must thrive.
From dusk until dawn, let our hearts take flight,
In this symphony of joy, we find pure delight.

Moonlit Mischief

In the silver glow, where secrets reside,
Moonlit mischief beckons, the stars as our guide.
With laughter we wander, in shadows of glow,
Creating our tales, in the soft evening flow.

A sprinkle of starlight, a dash of pure fun,
Playing hide and seek, with the moon and the sun.
In the cool midnight air, we chase down our dreams,
As giggles erupt, like soft whispering streams.

Reveling in moonbeams, we dance on the grass,
Each step a reminder, that moments can pass.
In the magic of night, we play without care,
Moonlit mischief thrumming, in the cool evening air.

So let us embrace this wild, carefree play,
Under the moon's watchful eye, come what may.
For the night is our canvas, painted in light,
With mischief and magic, we'll cherish this night.

Starlight Serenades

In the hush of night, we sway,
Under the moon's soft embrace.
Whispers of dreams drift away,
In starlit calm, we find our grace.

Crickets sing their lullabies,
While shadows dance on the ground.
The universe in quiet sighs,
In this moment, peace is found.

Flickering lights across the dark,
Paint tales of love in the air.
Hearts are ignited, a bright spark,
In night's embrace, we lay bare.

A serenade to the divine,
With each twinkle, hopes arise.
Lost in the rhythm of time,
Beneath the vast, eternal skies.

Giggling Stars in the Velvet Sky

Laughter echoes through the night,
As stars play hide and seek above.
Their twinkling forms, a playful sight,
Whispering tales of dream and love.

In velvet skies, they leap and gleam,
Casting smiles on those who gaze.
Their giggles weave a silken dream,
In the starlight's gentle haze.

The moon grins wide, a watchful eye,
As constellations dance and sway.
Each sparkle tells a story nigh,
Of ancient worlds in bright display.

So let us join this cosmic play,
With laughter bright to light our way.
Under the stars, we'll always stay,
In joy's embrace, forever gay.

Evening's Joyful Awakening

As day departs, the sky ignites,
With hues of orange, gold, and red.
The sun bows low in farewell lights,
While twilight whispers soft instead.

A chorus of the night begins,
With crickets chirping, frogs in song.
The world awakens to its spins,
In evening's glow, where hearts belong.

The stars like lanterns twinkle bright,
A symphony that calls us near.
We watch the dance of day and night,
In harmony, devoid of fear.

Each moment cherished, breathing deep,
In this embrace, we find our peace.
As darkness lingers, dreams take leap,
In evening's joy, we find release.

Frolics Beneath the Cosmic Canopy

Underneath the cosmic sheet,
We twirl and spin with pure delight.
The stars above, our hearts do greet,
In a dance of dreams throughout the night.

Galaxies swirl in endless flight,
While whispers of stardust fill the air.
We laugh with every twinkling light,
In frolics that banish every care.

The Milky Way trails a silver thread,
As shadows play upon the ground.
With open hearts, we leap ahead,
In the cosmic magic that surrounds.

So let us roam 'neath this grand dome,
Embraced by all that we can see.
In the universe, we find our home,
In joyful frolic, wild and free.

Twilight's Playful Spirit

In the sky, colors blend,
As day and night softly mend.
Whispers dance on the breeze,
Nature's lullaby, sweet with ease.

Beneath the trees, shadows play,
Chasing the light at end of day.
Stars begin to twinkle bright,
In the magic of twilight's light.

Along the path, laughter flows,
Carried where the moonlight glows.
Each moment sings, pure delight,
A serenade to the night.

Twilight's spirit, wild and free,
Invites us all to simply be.
In its embrace, we find our part,
Uniting souls with joyful heart.

Laughter Echoes in the Silence

In the quiet, giggles rise,
Filling space with soft surprise.
Echoes dance on the evening air,
Whispers blend, each laugh a prayer.

Moments shared, so precious, bright,
Bringing warmth within the night.
Softy shared secrets reside,
In the stillness, joy can't hide.

Every chuckle, every grin,
Threads of joy woven thin.
In the silence, hearts align,
Finding solace in the divine.

Laughter together, a sweet refrain,
Healing wounds, easing the pain.
In soft echoes, love's embrace,
We find our way, we find our place.

The Jester of Nightfall

At the dusk, a figure twirls,
A jester juggles, laughter swirls.
With a cap of bright, bold hues,
He dances free, banishing blues.

His floppy shoes tap on the ground,
In every flip, pure joy is found.
With a wink and a playful grin,
He draws us close, invites us in.

Under stars, he spins his tales,
Of moonlit rivers and gentle gales.
In his antics, time stands still,
With every laugh, we feel the thrill.

The jester of night, with charm so pure,
In a world of magic, we are sure.
As laughter echoes, shadows flee,
In his presence, we are free.

Playful Shadows and Laughing Lights

In the twilight, shadows creep,
Playing softly, secrets keep.
Laughing lights dance on the ground,
A vibrant symphony, joyous sound.

As stars emerge, they twinkle bright,
Guiding dreams in the soft night.
Playful shadows stretch and sway,
As magic weaves in a gentle play.

Beneath the moon, a blanket spread,
Echoes of laughter, softly fed.
In the dance of light and shade,
Every moment, joy cascades.

Embrace the night, let spirits soar,
In playful shadows, we explore.
With light and laughter intertwined,
We find the treasures of our mind.

The Joyful Spirit of Dusk

The day gives way to twilight's serenade,
Soft whispers linger in the fading light.
Colors dance upon the horizon displayed,
Nature sighs softly at the beauty in sight.

Fireflies emerge to twinkle and glide,
Painting portraits of dreams in the air.
The gentle breeze becomes a trusted guide,
Carrying secrets only night can bear.

Stars awaken, twinkling above,
As if to join in the evening's delight.
Moonlight spills like an embrace of love,
Wrapping the world in its silvery light.

Joyful spirits roam in the night's gentle grasp,
Celebrating the wonders we often dismiss.
In dusk's tender arms, we learn to unclasp,
Finding peace in the echoes of bliss.

Dreamy Echoes of the Night

In the quiet heart of the moonlit expanse,
Whispers of dreams begin to emerge.
Each sigh of the night holds a delicate chance,
To dance through the shadows where hopes surge.

Stars hum a melody sweet to behold,
Stories of wanderers lost in their quest.
With every twinkle, a memory retold,
Lost in the magic, the soul finds its rest.

Clouds drift lazily, forming soft shapes,
A canvas of wonders across the vast sky.
In the stillness, imagination escapes,
As night fills the air with serene lullaby.

Echoes of dreams paint the dark with delight,
Cradled in comfort, one's spirit can soar.
Awakening to the whispers of night,
We find our place, forever wanting more.

Laughter's Glow in the Darkness

In the depths of night where shadows reside,
Laughter spills forth like a fountain of light.
A melody sweet that joy will not hide,
Guiding the hearts that embrace the night.

Whimsical tales woven with glee,
Crisp echoes ring in the cool, soft embrace.
Bantering voices like waves on the sea,
Lift spirits high in this warm, sacred space.

Glimmers of joy spark in each gentle jest,
Lighting the dark like a beacon so bright.
Moments together, we cherish the best,
In laughter's warm glow, we conquer the night.

As starlight winks and the moon shares its beams,
We find our solace in this festive cheer.
In darkness, we weave the most wonderful dreams,
Laughter's embrace ever charming and near.

Enigmatic Chuckles of the Night

Beneath the velvet sky, secrets play,
Mysterious chuckles echo through the dark.
In shadows, they dance and sway,
Leaving behind just a trace, a spark.

Each laugh carries hints of untold tales,
A riddle woven in the still, cool air.
Wandering whispers like gentle gales,
Curious minds drift, eager to share.

With every chuckle, the night seems alive,
Entwining stories where reality bends.
Enticing the dreamers, our spirits revive,
Inviting the jesters, the night never ends.

Enigmatic laughter wraps around the soul,
Authentic connections that keep us awake.
In the heart of the night, we are made whole,
Within these chuckles, new worlds we create.

Dusk's Mischievous Twinkle

As twilight drapes the skies so wide,
The stars emerge, like whispers shy.
They flicker, dance with playful pride,
In secrets shared as night draws nigh.

The moonlight spills on silver streams,
Casting shadows, soft and low.
A world alive with twinkling dreams,
Where magic thrives in evening's glow.

Glimmers tease the sleepy trees,
With laughter riding on the breeze.
The velvet night, a canvas bright,
Where mischief brews beneath the light.

As dusk unfolds its charm so sweet,
Each twinkling star a tiny greet.
In playful jest, they take their flight,
A wondrous sight, a pure delight.

The Playhouse of the Night

In the shadows, dreams take stage,
With actors clad in robes of night.
The stars, the audience, engage,
While owls hoot soft, their wings in flight.

A whisper here, a giggle there,
The moonbeam dances, casting glow.
From velvet drapes, secrets flare,
As night unfolds its wondrous show.

In corners dark, where stories bloom,
The laughter weaves through open space.
The crickets hum a sweetened tune,
As dreams awaken, start to chase.

The playhouse thrives with nightly cheer,
Where whimsy reigns, and hearts draw near.
A tapestry of tales retold,
In every shadow, magic bold.

Midnight Giggles Among the Stars

When midnight falls, the stars align,
They giggle softly, twinkling bright.
In playful jest, they seem to shine,
A secret world just out of sight.

The cosmos whispers, laughter sweet,
As shadows stretch, the night takes flight.
Each twinkle holds a tale complete,
As dreams unfold beneath the light.

A cosmic dance, a playful game,
With laughter echoing through the dark.
Each star a friend, no two the same,
And all together, they leave a mark.

In midnight's glow, the giggles rise,
A symphony beneath the skies.
In every heartbeat, joy resides,
As night reveals its sweet surprise.

The Festival of Nocturnal Whimsy

Beneath the moon, the fairies play,
In hidden nooks, they spin and sway.
With laughter bright, they light the night,
In charming tales of pure delight.

The owls, they hoot a merry tune,
While shadows move and softly swoon.
The stars, like lanterns, shine above,
As creatures gather, full of love.

A festival, where dreams take flight,
In gentle whispers, hearts unite.
The night reveals its timeless grace,
Where whimsy dances, setting pace.

In moments shared, the magic's clear,
As joy unfolds in night, so dear.
Come join the merry, twinkling stream,
A nocturnal festival of dreams.

Echoes of Fun in the Shadows

In the twilight where shadows blend,
Laughter dances, a playful trend.
Echoes whisper secrets anew,
Reveling in joy, just me and you.

With each giggle, the night unfolds,
Stories whispered, laughter bold.
Stars above, our silent crowd,
In shadows deep, we're lost, unbowed.

Crickets chirp, a rhythmic song,
Playful spirits where we belong.
In the stillness, joy ignites,
Echoes of fun on these starry nights.

As the moonlight paints the skies,
We chase dreams, where laughter flies.
In every echo, a spark we find,
Echoes of fun, forever intertwined.

The Night's Gentle Giggle

When the moonlight starts to gleam,
The night unfolds like a tender dream.
A gentle giggle fills the air,
Whispers of magic, light as a prayer.

Beneath the stars, shadows sway,
In the quiet, we laugh and play.
Silvery beams on our faces glow,
The night hums softly, sweet and slow.

In every rustle, a secret shared,
In nighttime's charm, we are ensnared.
Each giggle echoing through the trees,
A dance of laughter in the soothing breeze.

As dreams drift in on velvet wings,
The night composes its gentle sings.
With every heartbeat, joy runs free,
The night's soft giggle belongs to thee.

Whispers of Laughter in the Darkness

In the shadows where secrets lie,
Laughter whispers, a sweet reply.
Moonbeams flicker on hidden trails,
While joy in darkness softly sails.

Through the night, echoes collide,
With every chuckle, we take a ride.
In hushed corners, mischief brews,
Laughter dances, the dark renews.

Every giggle, a fleeting spark,
Lighting the edges of the dark.
With whispers low, our spirits soar,
In the dark, we find even more.

As night wraps us in its embrace,
We share our dreams in this sacred space.
Laughter lingers, forever it clings,
In whispers of joy, our heartstrings sing.

A Symphony of Night's Laughter

In the night, a symphony plays,
Soft laughter weaving through the maze.
Each note dances on the breeze,
Creating melodies that tease.

With stars as our shimmering guide,
We let the night's laughter abide.
Every chuckle a story told,
In this symphony, brave and bold.

From the shadows, joy takes flight,
In the depth of the starry night.
Whispers of giggles float aloft,
A lively sound, uplifting and soft.

As crickets join in humble tune,
The night awakens, a playful boon.
Together we dance, hearts intertwine,
In this night's laughter, we boldly shine.

Celestial Chuckles

Stars twinkle bright, a playful jest,
Moonlight dances, a silvery crest.
Laughing clouds roll in the night,
Whispers of joy, a pure delight.

Comets race, a fleeting grin,
Galaxies spin, the dreams begin.
In the vastness, giggles hum,
A cosmic show, the night-time fun.

Planets twirl in rhythm's embrace,
Celestial bodies, a lively chase.
Each twinkling light, a chuckling spark,
In the universe's laughter, we find our mark.

Eclipses play, a curtain call,
As starlit laughter fills the hall.
Beyond the space, where dreams reside,
Celestial chuckles, a joy-filled ride.

The Night's Secret Comedy

The moon grins wide, a cheeky moon,
Crickets chirp, a midnight tune.
Fireflies flicker, a light tease,
In the dark, the shadows freeze.

Starlit jokes upon the breeze,
Whispers shared among the trees.
The night unveils her playful mask,
In quiet corners, secrets bask.

Laughter flows from distant shores,
As night unveils its hidden stores.
With every blink, a laugh takes flight,
In the gallery of the starlit night.

A playful breeze steals the sighs,
Under the stretch of velvet skies.
The night's a stage, we all are cast,
In this comedy, forever vast.

Prances of Joy in Dusk's Veil

When the day bows down to night,
Joy prances in fading light.
Colors blend in warm embrace,
Nature's canvas, a vibrant space.

The sun dips low, a golden tease,
Wind sings soft, a gentle breeze.
Whispers float on twilight's breath,
In dusk's veil, we find our depth.

Crickets join in the evening song,
As shadows stretch, where we belong.
Laughter mingles with the sigh,
In this moment, we learn to fly.

The stars awake, a twinkling cheer,
In quiet joy, we hold them near.
Prances of joy, the heart feels free,
In dusk's warm veil, just you and me.

Smiles Under the Celestial Dome

Under the dome of the vast expanse,
Stars invite us to take a chance.
With every light, a smile ignites,
A tapestry woven in magical nights.

The moon winks down, a playful glance,
As we twirl in this cosmic dance.
Heartbeats sync with the universe's tune,
In the rhythm of night, we find our boon.

Galaxies swirl, a joyful spree,
Each star a wink, a spark of glee.
Together we bask in this dazzling sight,
With smiles that shine, we ignite the night.

Underneath this celestial glow,
United in laughter, we let it flow.
With every breath, the magic roams,
In smiles shared, we call this home.

Whimsical Whispers of Dusk

Whispers float as daylight fades,
Softly painted in twilight shades.
A gentle breeze begins to play,
As colors dance at end of day.

Stars peek through the velvet sky,
Each one gleaming, a twinkling sigh.
Dreams awaken, take their flight,
In the hush of approaching night.

Moonlight bathes the world in gold,
Stories of the night unfold.
Crickets sing their evening tune,
As fireflies flicker like tiny moons.

In this magic, hearts unite,
Bathed in the soft embrace of night.
The world is wrapped in mystic grace,
A sacred, timeless, tranquil space.

Laughter's Hidden Pathways

Footsteps echo down the lane,
Where laughter dances, free of pain.
Each corner hides a joyful sound,
In the places where friends are found.

With whispers sweet and giggles bright,
They weave the fabric of the night.
Together sharing, spirits soar,
In every moment, craving more.

Joy's essence is found in play,
In every silly game we sway.
With hearts so light, we chase the fun,
Creating memories, one by one.

A treasure trove of playful dreams,
In laughter's embrace, life gleams.
Through hidden paths, we find our way,
In love and laughter, we will stay.

Joyful Shadows in the Quiet Dark

In the quiet, shadows glide,
With gentle whispers, they confide.
Softly cupping dreams anew,
In the stillness, hearts break through.

Each shadow dances, light unfurls,
Creating pictures of distant worlds.
Laughter echoes through the night,
Filling spaces with pure delight.

Beneath the stars, we come alive,
In twilight's grace, we freely thrive.
Joyful moments, hand in hand,
In the dark, we boldly stand.

The moon's soft glow, a guiding spark,
To ignite our lives when life feels dark.
Together, we'll weave our sweet refrain,
In joyful shadows, we'll dance again.

Starlit Reverie of Playful Spirits

Under starlit skies, we dream,
In the space where wishes beam.
Playful spirits glide and soar,
In this realm, we seek for more.

With laughter bright as shooting stars,
We build our dreams, forget our scars.
Every twinkle tells a tale,
Of heartbeats strong that will prevail.

In night's embrace, we find our muse,
To write the songs our hearts will choose.
On starlit paths, we dance along,
Where every moment feels like a song.

Together in this cosmic dance,
We capture time, we seize the chance.
In reverie of light so pure,
Our spirit's joy will ever endure.

Secrets of the Midnight Breeze

Whispers drift on gentle air,
Secrets shared with silvery flair.
Underneath the starry dome,
Lost in tales of night, we roam.

Footsteps light on dew-kissed grass,
Moments fleeting, yet they last.
Every sigh a hidden thought,
In the stillness, dreams are caught.

Echoes linger of what's past,
Messages the shadows cast.
Breezes play a soft refrain,
In their dance, love's sweet remain.

Hearts align beneath the moon,
Softly humming a familiar tune.
Through the night, we feel so free,
Embraced by the midnight spree.

Echoes of Mirth at Dusk

In twilight's glow, laughter swells,
Echoes trickle, gentle bells.
Children's giggles fill the air,
Dancing shadows everywhere.

Sunset paints the sky with cheer,
Moments cherished, gathered near.
Whispers soft as voices blend,
At dusk's gate, good times extend.

Flickering lights, a warm embrace,
Inviting smiles on every face.
Life's sweet melody unfolds,
In the sweetest stories told.

With each breath, the heart beats strong,
In this symphony, we belong.
Echoes of joy stretch high above,
In the twilight's embrace of love.

Shadows Tickling the Heart

Soft shadows dance in fading light,
Caressing dreams that feel so right.
Each heartbeat whispers tales untold,
Secrets linger, brave and bold.

A playful nudge, a fleeting glance,
Hearts entwined, lost in romance.
Shadows linger, a gentle tease,
Resting lightly like a breeze.

Moments fleeting, forever near,
Tickling hearts with gentle cheer.
Silhouettes in the twilight glow,
Reminders of love's sweet flow.

In the dim, connections spark,
Guided softly through the dark.
Shadows blend with the beating heart,
In this dance, we'll never part.

Playful Dreams in Twilight's Embrace

In twilight's arms, where dreams arise,
Playfulness dances in the skies.
Colors swirl in a vivid spin,
Whimsical journeys wait within.

Imagination takes its flight,
On the wings of fading light.
Every thought a spark, a flame,
In the night, we find our name.

Softly spoken, secrets shared,
In this moment, we are spared.
Wisps of joy, like fragile threads,
Sewing paths where laughter spreads.

Hold my hand and close your eyes,
Let's paint the world with sweet surprise.
In playful dreams, forever stay,
Twilight's embrace, our hearts at play.

Spinning Tales in the Midnight Hour

In shadows deep, the stories flow,
Whispers soft, where secrets glow.
Under stars, our dreams take flight,
Spinning tales in the velvet night.

Moonbeams dance on silent streams,
Echoes linger, chase our dreams.
With every word, the magic swells,
In this hour, where magic dwells.

Forgotten tales of long ago,
In candlelight, their glories show.
We gather close, our hearts entwined,
In midnight tales, new worlds we find.

As dawn begins to steal the show,
We hold our breath, reluctance grow.
With every story, time does pause,
In that hour, we find our cause.

Midnight Chortles

Laughter bubbles in the night,
Stars above, they shine so bright.
Whimsical tales spin like a kite,
Midnight chortles, pure delight.

Tickling dreams in a quiet space,
Giggles echo, soft embrace.
The moon joins in, a kindred sprite,
In our laughter, hearts take flight.

Whispers share the sweetest jest,
In this hour, we feel so blessed.
With each chuckle, worries ease,
Midnight magic, winds that tease.

But as the hour starts to wane,
We promise to meet here again.
For laughter shared is never lost,
In midnight chortles, we count the cost.

The Celestial Playground

Above the world, where dreams are spun,
Planets play, and stars do run.
Galaxies twirl in cosmic play,
In the celestial playground, night and day.

Nebulas bloom in colors bright,
Drawing eyes in wondrous sight.
Asteroids dance in a graceful line,
Through the cosmos, where stardust shines.

Time stands still in the vast expanse,
Comets drift in their timeless dance.
The universe sings a serenade,
In this playground, joy is made.

As we gaze upon the night sky,
We feel our spirits start to fly.
With every dream that's spun anew,
The celestial playground welcomes you.

Frolicking Fantasies at Sundown

As daylight fades, the colors gleam,
Frolicking fantasies, like a dream.
Shadows stretch, the world aglow,
At sundown's touch, imagination flows.

The horizon wears a golden crown,
While laughter echoes through the town.
Children play in fields so wide,
With every giggle, joy and pride.

Fireflies flicker in the dusk's embrace,
Guiding us to a magic place.
With every wink, the night unfolds,
In frolicking fantasies, tales are told.

As the stars twinkle bright and clear,
We hold our dreams, we hold them near.
In this moment, we are free,
Frolicking in dreams, just you and me.

Milton Keynes UK
Ingram Content Group UK Ltd.
UKHW021928011224
451790UK00005B/73